"Be beautiful in your heart
by being gentle and quiet.
This kind of beauty will last,
and God considers it very special."

To:

Emma

From:

Daddy

Date:

June 30, 2012

Little Miss Grace™ Promise Book

© 2009 Christian Art Gifts, RSA
       Christian Art Gifts Inc., IL, USA

Designed by Christian Art Gifts

Printed in China

ISBN 978-1-77036-247-5

11 12 13 14 15 16 17 18 19 20 – 17 16 15 14 13 12 11 10 9 8

Little Miss Grace™

Promise
Book

christian
art gifts®

Contents

Little Miss Grace ...

Little Miss Grace ...

Is Gracious

God puts words of grace and
beauty on display.

Proverbs 15:26 THE MESSAGE

Be beautiful in your heart by being gentle
and quiet. This kind of beauty will last,
and God considers it very special.

1 Peter 3:4 CEV

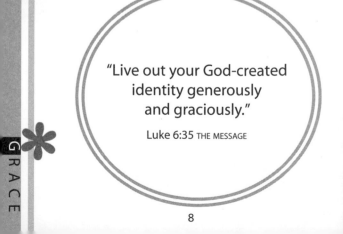

"Live out your God-created
identity generously
and graciously."

Luke 6:35 THE MESSAGE

GRACE

The words of a wise person
are gracious.

Ecclesiastes 10:12 THE MESSAGE

Whoever loves a pure heart and
gracious speech will have the
king as a friend.

Proverbs 22:11 NLT

The LORD your God is gracious.
He will not turn His face from you.

2 Chronicles 30:9 NLT

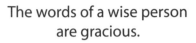

GRACE

9

How kind the LORD is!
How good He is!
So merciful, this God of ours!

Psalm 116:5 NLT

God taught us to give up our
worldly desires and to live decent
and honest lives in this world.

Titus 2:12 CEV

Clothe yourselves with
tenderhearted mercy, kindness,
humility, gentleness, and patience.

Colossians 3:12 NLT

GRACE

Whenever we are in need,
we should come bravely before the
throne of our merciful God. There we
will be treated with undeserved
kindness, and we will find help.

Hebrews 4:16 CEV

From His abundance we have
all received one gracious
blessing after another.

John 1:16 NLT

Grace is God's
love and mercy
reaching others
through you.

GRACE

Little Miss Grace ...

Gives Glory to God

Give glory to GOD.

Joshua 7:19 THE MESSAGE

He is the only God, the One who saves us.
To Him be glory, greatness, power, and
authority through Jesus Christ our Lord
for all time past, now, and forever.

Jude 25 NCV

Our Lord and God, You are worthy to
receive glory, honor, and power.
You created all things.

Revelation 4:11 CEV

GRACE

The LORD is great and deserves our greatest praise! He is the only God worthy of our worship.

1 Chronicles 16:25 CEV

You are wonderful, LORD, and You deserve all praise, because You are much greater than anyone can understand.

Psalm 145:3 CEV

Sing praises to the Lord, praise His holy name.

Psalm 30:4 NCV

GRACE

This is the day that the LORD
has made. Let us rejoice and
be glad today!

Psalm 118:24 NCV

Let's praise God! He listened
when I prayed, and He is
always kind.

Psalm 66:20 CEV

"Rejoice and be glad, because you have a
great reward waiting for you in heaven."

Matthew 5:12 NCV

The godly will rejoice in the LORD
and find shelter in Him.

Psalm 64:10 NLT

Graceful girls glorify
God every day!

Is Generous

God loves a person who
gives cheerfully.

2 Corinthians 9:7 NLT

Generous hands are blessed hands.

Proverbs 22:9 THE MESSAGE

The generous will prosper;
those who refresh others will
themselves be refreshed.

Proverbs 11:25 NLT

Give generously to the poor,
not grudgingly, for the L\ord your God
will bless you in everything you do.

Deuteronomy 15:10 NLT

"Give, and you will receive. Your gift
will return to you in full."

Luke 6:38 NLT

Give to everyone what you owe them.

Romans 13:7 NLT

Each of you must make up your own mind about how much to give. But don't feel sorry that you must give and don't feel that you are forced to give. God loves people who love to give. God can bless you with everything you need, and you will always have more than enough to do all kinds of good things for others.

2 Corinthians 9:7-8 CEV

Whoever gives to the poor will lack nothing.

Proverbs 28:27 NLT

GRACE

Give your food to the hungry
and care for the homeless.

Isaiah 58:10 CEV

Be generous, and someday
you will be rewarded.

Ecclesiastes 11:1 CEV

Teach us to use wisely all
the time we have.

Psalm 90:12 CEV

Giving is a privilege –
not a duty.

GRACE

Little Miss Grace ...

Each of you has been blessed with one of
God's many wonderful gifts to be used in
the service of others. So use your gift well.

1 Peter 4:10 CEV

Christ gave each one of us the special gift
of grace, showing how generous He is.

Ephesians 4:7 NCV

God has given each of us different gifts to use

Romans 12:6 CEV

Every good action and every
perfect gift is from God.

James 1:17 NCV

God has given us the Holy Spirit, who
fills our hearts with His love.

Romans 5:5 CEV

"To those who use well what they are
given, even more will be given,
and they will have an abundance."

Matthew 25:29 NLT

We don't have the right to claim that
we have done anything on our own.
God gives us what it takes to do all
that we do.

2 Corinthians 3:5 CEV

GRACE

God blesses His loyal people.

Proverbs 28:20 CEV

If you have the gift of speaking,
preach God's message. If you have the
gift of helping others, do it with the
strength that God supplies.

1 Peter 4:11 CEV

Respect and serve the LORD!
Your reward will be wealth,
a long life, and honor.

Proverbs 22:4 CEV

GRACE

There are different kinds of
spiritual gifts, but the same Spirit
is the source of them all. There are
different kinds of service, but we
serve the same Lord. God works in
different ways, but it is the same
God who does the work in all of us.
A spiritual gift is given to each of us
so we can help each other.

1 Corinthians 12:4-7 NLT

God blesses everyone
with special gifts and
talents. He created
everyone to shine!

GRACE

Is Good-Hearted

The Holy Spirit produces
this kind of fruit in our lives:
love, joy, peace, patience, kindness,
goodness, faithfulness, gentleness,
and self-control. There is no law
against these things!

Galatians 5:22-23 NLT

Jesus Christ will keep you busy
doing good deeds that bring
glory and praise to God.

Philippians 1:11 CEV

GRACE

All who do right will be
rewarded with glory,
honor, and peace.

Romans 2:10 CEV

We must not become tired of doing good.
We will receive our harvest of eternal life at
the right time if we do not give up.

Galatians 6:9 NCV

Always be humble, gentle, and patient,
accepting each other in love.

Ephesians 4:2 NCV

GRACE

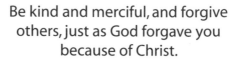

Be kind and merciful, and forgive others, just as God forgave you because of Christ.

Ephesians 4:32 CEV

She must also be well known for doing all sorts of good things, such as giving food to strangers, helping people in need, and always making herself useful.

1 Timothy 5:10 CEV

"A good person produces good things
from the treasury of a good heart."

Matthew 12:35 NLT

Good people will prosper like palm trees,
and they will grow strong.

Psalm 92:12 CEV

I long to obey Your commandments!
Renew my life with Your goodness.

Psalm 119:40 NLT

No act of kindness, no matter
how small, is ever wasted.

~ Aesop

GRACE

Little Miss Grace ...

Grows Spiritually

Grow in the grace and knowledge of
our Lord and Savior Jesus Christ.

2 Peter 3:18 NCV

God is the One who began
this good work in you, and
I am certain that He won't
stop before it is complete.

Philippians 1:6 CEV

"I will bless those who trust Me.
They will be like trees growing
beside a stream."

Jeremiah 17:7-8 CEV

Be strong in the Lord and
in His mighty power.

Ephesians 6:10 NLT

Do your best to improve your faith.
You can do this by adding goodness,
understanding, self-control, patience,
devotion to God, concern for others,
and love. If you keep growing in this
way, it will show that what you know
about our Lord Jesus Christ has made
your lives useful and meaningful.

2 Peter 1:5-8 CEV

GRACE

I ask the Father in His great glory to give you the power to be strong inwardly through His Spirit.

Ephesians 3:16 NCV

Be like newborn babies who are thirsty for the pure spiritual milk that will help you grow and be saved.

1 Peter 2:2 CEV

We live by every word that comes from GOD's mouth.

Deuteronomy 8:3 THE MESSAGE

Always pray that God will show you everything He wants you to do and that you may have all the wisdom and understanding that His Spirit gives.

Colossians 1:9 CEV

Train yourself to serve God. Training your body helps you in some ways, but serving God helps you in every way by bringing you blessings in this life and in the future life, too.

1 Timothy 4:7-8 NCV

Let the Word grow you into the person God created you to be.

GRACE

R

"You should be a light for other people. Live so that they will see the good things you do and will praise your Father in heaven."

Matthew 5:16 NCV

Do not let anyone treat you as if you are unimportant because you are young. Instead, be an example to the believers with your words, your actions, your love, your faith, and your pure life.

1 Timothy 4:12 NCV

GRACE

The ways of right-living people glow
with light; the longer they live,
the brighter they shine.

Proverbs 4:18 THE MESSAGE

"You are like light for the whole
world. A city built on top of a hill
cannot be hidden, and no one
would light a lamp and put it
under a clay pot. A lamp is placed
on a lampstand, where it can give
light to everyone in the house."

Matthew 5:14-15 CEV

They will be so kind and merciful
and good, that they will be a
light in the dark for others
who do the right thing.

Psalm 112:4 CEV

GRACE

If we live in the light, as God is in the light, we can share fellowship with each other.

1 John 1:7 NCV

Do everything without complaining or arguing. Then you will be innocent and without any wrong. You will be God's children without fault. But you are living with crooked and mean people all around you, among whom you shine like stars in the dark world.

Philippians 2:14-15 NCV

Live such good lives that people will see the good things you do and will give glory to God on the day when Christ comes again.

1 Peter 2:12 NCV

GRACE

You are God's special people. God has brought you out of darkness into His marvelous light. Now you must tell all the wonderful things that He has done.

1 Peter 2:9 CEV

"I am the light for the world! Follow Me, and you won't be walking in the dark. You will have the light that gives life."

John 8:12 CEV

Our faces, then, are not covered. We all show the Lord's glory.

2 Corinthians 3:18 NCV

All the darkness of the world cannot put out the light of one small candle.

~ Anonymous

Reaches Out

Two people are better off than one, for they can help each other succeed. If one person falls, the other can reach out and help.

Ecclesiastes 4:9-10 NLT

"Love your neighbor as yourself."

Luke 10:27 NLT

If we have all we need and see one of our own people in need, we must have pity on that person, or else we cannot say we love God. Children, you show love for others by truly helping them, and not merely by talking about it.

1 John 3:17-18 CEV

GRACE

If you know someone who doesn't have any clothes or food, you shouldn't just say, "I hope all goes well for you. I hope you will be warm and have plenty to eat." What good is it to say this, unless you do something to help? Faith that doesn't lead us to do good deeds is all alone and dead!

James 2:15-17 CEV

"Be kind and merciful to one another!"

Zechariah 7:8 CEV

"Have pity on others, just as your Father has pity on you."

Luke 6:36 CEV

GRACE

"Ask yourself what you want people to do for you, then grab the initiative and do it for them."

Matthew 7:12 THE MESSAGE

"You should be fair and kind to others."

Luke 11:42 CEV

Be happy with those who are happy, and be sad with those who are sad.

Romans 12:15 NCV

GRACE

"Love your enemies
and be good to them
Lend without expecting to
be paid back. Then you will
get a great reward, and you
will be the true children
of God in heaven."

Luke 6:35 CEV

There is no exercise better
for the heart than reaching down
and lifting someone else up.

~ Anonymous

GRACE

Reaches Up

This I declare about the Lord:
He is my God, and I trust Him.

Psalm 91:2 NLT

I trust in the Lord with all my heart.

Psalm 28:7 NLT

Let's come near God with pure hearts
and a confidence that comes
from having faith.

Hebrews 10:22 CEV

GRACE

Have faith in the Lord Jesus
and you will be saved!

Acts 16:31 CEV

The fundamental fact of
existence is that this trust in God,
this faith, is the firm foundation
under everything that makes
life worth living.

Hebrews 11:1 THE MESSAGE

GRACE

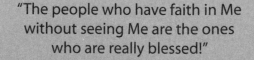

"The people who have faith in Me
without seeing Me are the ones
who are really blessed!"

John 20:29 CEV

God can always be trusted.

Deuteronomy 32:4 CEV

"Anything is possible if
a person believes."

Mark 9:23 NLT

GRACE

44

When your faith remains strong
through trials, it will bring
you much praise and
glory and honor.

1 Peter 1:7 NLT

We live by believing and
not by seeing.

2 Corinthians 5:7 NLT

When God is your
best friend, the days are
brighter and filled with
His blessings.

Is Respectful

Honor your father and mother.

Exodus 20:12 NLT

"Show respect to the aged;
honor the presence of an elder;
fear your God. I am GOD."

Leviticus 19:32 THE MESSAGE

Obey your parents in all things,
because this pleases the Lord.

Colossians 3:20 NCV

GRACE

Don't be selfish; don't try to impress others.
Be humble, thinking of others as better
than yourselves. Don't look out only
for your own interests, but take an
interest in others, too.

Philippians 2:3 4 NLT

Love others as you love yourself.

James 2:8 THE MESSAGE

Respect everyone and show
special love for God's people.

1 Peter 2:17 CEV

G
R
A
C
E

47

Love from the center of who you are;
don't fake it. Run for dear life from evil;
hold on for dear life to good. Be good
friends who love deeply; practice
playing second fiddle.

Romans 12:9-10 THE MESSAGE

A kind woman gets respect.

Proverbs 11:16 NCV

"If you humble yourself,
you will be honored."

Luke 14:11 CEV

Take delight in honoring each other.

Romans 12:10 NLT

GRACE

"Do not worship any god except Me.
Don't bow down and worship idols.
I am the LORD your God,
and I demand all your love.
Do not misuse My name.
Remember that the
Sabbath Day belongs to Me.
Respect your father and your mother.
Do not murder. Be faithful in marriage.
Do not steal. Do not tell lies about others.
Do not want anything that belongs
to someone else."

Exodus 20:3-17 CEV

If you respect others
they will respect you.

GRACE

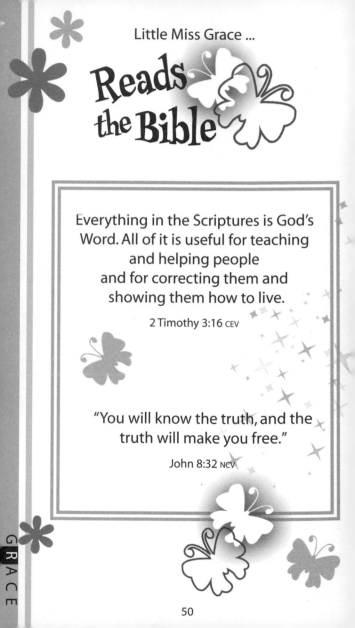

Reads the Bible

Everything in the Scriptures is God's Word. All of it is useful for teaching and helping people and for correcting them and showing them how to live.

2 Timothy 3:16 CEV

"You will know the truth, and the truth will make you free."

John 8:32 NCV

GRACE

Young people can live a clean life
by obeying Your word.

Psalm 119:9 CEV

Your word is a lamp that gives light
wherever I walk.

Psalm 119:105 CEV

"The people who are really blessed are the
ones who hear and obey God's message!"

Luke 11:28 CEV

GRACE

51

Your words came to me,
and I listened carefully to them.
Your words made me very happy.

Jeremiah 15:16 NCV

I treasure Your word
above all else.

Psalm 119:11 CEV

Your word is my source of hope.

Psalm 119:114 NLT

GRACE

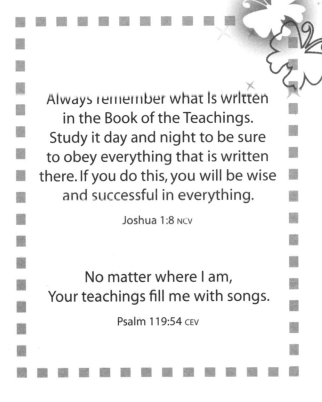

Always remember what is written
in the Book of the Teachings.
Study it day and night to be sure
to obey everything that is written
there. If you do this, you will be wise
and successful in everything.

Joshua 1:8 NCV

No matter where I am,
Your teachings fill me with songs.

Psalm 119:54 CEV

Avoid truth decay — read your Bible.

~ Anonymous

GRACE

53

Remembers to Pray

Do not worry about anything,
but pray and ask God for everything
you need, always giving thanks.
And God's peace, which is so great we
cannot understand it, will keep your
hearts and minds in Christ Jesus.

Philippians 4:6-7 NCV

Never stop praying, especially for others.
Always pray by the power of the Spirit.
Stay alert and keep praying for God's people.

Ephesians 6:18 CEV

Pray all the time.

1 Thessalonians 5:17 THE MESSAGE

GRACE

"Keep on asking,
and you will receive
what you ask for.
Keep on seeking,
and you will find.
Keep on knocking,
and the door will be opened"

Matthew 7:7 NLT

GRACE

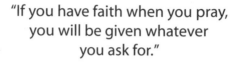

"If you have faith when you pray,
you will be given whatever
you ask for."

Matthew 21:22 CEV

Don't quit in hard times;
pray all the harder.

Romans 12:12 THE MESSAGE

When a believing person prays,
great things happen.

James 5:16 NCV

The Lord sees the good people and
listens to their prayers.

1 Peter 3:12 NCV

Don't worry about anything, but pray about
everything. With thankful hearts offer up
your prayers and requests to God.

Philippians 4:6 CEV

When you pray you are
whispering into God's ear.

GRACE

GRACE

Accepts Others

All of you should be in agreement, understanding each other, loving each other as family, being kind and humble.

1 Peter 3:8 NCV

"Don't pick on people, jump on their failures, criticize their faults – unless, of course, you want the same treatment. That critical spirit has a way of boomeranging. It's easy to see a smudge on your neighbor's face and be oblivious to the ugly sneer on your own."

Matthew 7:1-3 THE MESSAGE

We must stop judging others. We must also make up our minds not to upset anyone's faith.

Romans 14:13 CEV

GRACE

Don't say cruel things about others!
If you do, or if you condemn others,
you are condemning God's law. And if
you condemn the law, you put yourself
above the law and refuse to obey either
it or God who gave it. God is our judge.
What right do you have to condemn anyone?

James 4:11-12 CEV

"Looks aren't everything.
Don't be impressed with looks
and stature. GOD judges persons
differently than humans do.
Men and women look at the face;
GOD looks into the heart."

1 Samuel 16:7 THE MESSAGE

GRACE

Christ accepted you,
so you should accept each other,
which will bring glory to God.

Romans 15:7 NCV

Love each other.

1 Peter 1:22 NLT

Let us continue to love one another,
for love comes from God. Anyone who
loves is a child of God and knows God.

1 John 4:7 NLT

Be humble and give more honor to
others than to yourselves.

Philippians 2:3 NCV

GRACE

Kind words are like honey – sweet to
the soul and healthy for the body.

Proverbs 16:24 NLT

Make allowance for each other's faults,
and forgive anyone who offends you.
Remember, the Lord forgave you,
so you must forgive others. Above all,
clothe yourselves with love, which binds
us all together in perfect harmony.

Colossians 3:13-14 NLT

When you look for the
best in others, you bring out
the best in yourself.

Is Appreciative

Since everything God created is good, we should not reject any of it but receive it with thanks.

1 Timothy 4:4 NLT

Be cheerful no matter what; pray all the time; thank God no matter what happens. This is the way God wants you who belong to Christ Jesus to live.

1 Thessalonians 5:16-18 THE MESSAGE

GRACE

With all my heart I will thank the LORD when His people meet. The LORD has done many wonderful things!

Psalm 111:1-2 CEV

May you be filled with joy, always thanking the Father.

Colossians 1:11-12 NLT

GRACE

Tell the LORD how thankful you are,
because He is kind and always merciful.

Psalm 118:1 CEV

The LORD has done great things for us,
and we are very glad.

Psalm 126:3 NCV

Our God, we thank You for being so
near to us! Everyone celebrates
Your wonderful deeds.

Psalm 75:1 CEV

Lord, there is no god like You
and no works like Yours.

Psalm 86:8 NCV

You fill my cup until it overflows.
Your kindness and love
will always be with me
each day of my life.

Psalm 23:5-6 CEV

I am overwhelmed with joy in the LORD my God!

Isaiah 61:10 NLT

Take plenty of time to count your blessings,
but never spend a minute in worry.

~ Anonymous

GRACE

Is Amazing

I thank You, God –
You're breathtaking! Body and soul,
I am marvelously made!

Psalm 139:14 THE MESSAGE

We are God's masterpiece.

Ephesians 2:10 NLT

God brings the best out of you.

Romans 12:2 THE MESSAGE

Don't depend on things like
fancy hairdos or gold jewelry
or expensive clothes to
make you look beautiful.
Be beautiful in your heart
by being gentle and quiet.
This kind of beauty will last,
and God considers it very special.

1 Peter 3:3-4 CEV

Charm can mislead and beauty
soon fades. The woman to be
admired and praised is the woman
who lives in the Fear-of-God.
Give her everything she deserves!

Proverbs 31:30-31 THE MESSAGE

"God pays even greater attention to you –
down to the last detail."

Luke 12:7 THE MESSAGE

GRACE

God,
You are our Father.
We're the clay and
You're our potter:
All of us are what
You made us.

Isaiah 64:8 THE MESSAGE

Body and soul,
I am marvelously made!
You know me inside and out,
You know every bone in my body;
You know exactly how I was made,
bit by bit, how I was sculpted from
nothing into something.

Psalm 139:14-15 THE MESSAGE

GRACE

I can do everything through
Christ, who gives me strength.

Philippians 4:13 NLT

As cheese is made from milk,
You created my body from a tiny drop.

Job 10:10 CEV

Within you, just waiting to blossom,
is the wonderful promise of
all that you can be.

GRACE

Is Affectionate

Love never gives up.
Love cares more for others than for self.
Love isn't always "me first",
doesn't keep score of the sins of others,
puts up with anything,
trusts God always,
always looks for the best,
never looks back,
but keeps going to the end.

1 Corinthians 13:4-7 THE MESSAGE

GRACE

Do everything with love.

1 Corinthians 16:14 NLT

Love each other deeply
with all your heart.

1 Peter 1:22 NLT

Love will last forever!

1 Corinthians 13:8 NLT

Live a life filled with love.

Ephesians 5:2 NLT

Most important of all, you must
sincerely love each other.

1 Peter 4:8 CEV

Pursue righteous living,
faithfulness, love, and peace.
Enjoy the companionship
of those who call on the Lord
with pure hearts.

2 Timothy 2:22 NLT

Let us continue to love one another,
for love comes from God. Anyone
who loves is a child of God
and knows God.

1 John 4:7 NLT

Bless – that's your job, to bless.
You'll be a blessing and also
get a blessing.

1 Peter 3:9 THE MESSAGE

"Love your enemies. Help and give
without expecting a return. You'll never
regret it. Our Father is kind; you be kind."

Luke 6:35-36 THE MESSAGE

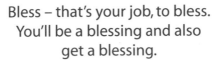

When you love
others, you make
their world a
little bit brighter.

Is Adopted

God was kind and
decided that Christ
would choose us
to be God's own
adopted children.

Ephesians 1:5 CEV

Think how much the Father loves us.
He loves us so much that He lets
us be called His children.

1 John 3:1 CEV

When I left the womb You cradled me;
since the moment of birth You've been my God.

Psalm 22:10 THE MESSAGE

"All who are victorious will inherit all
these blessings, and I will be their God,
and they will be My children."

Revelation 21:7 NLT

Those people who are led by God's Spirit
are His children.

Romans 8:14 CEV

Some people accepted Him and
put their faith in Him. So He gave them
the right to be the children of God.

John 1:12 CEV

GRACE

You are all children of God
through faith in Christ Jesus.

Galatians 3:26 NCV

God saved us, not because
of the righteous things we had
done, but because of His mercy.
He washed away our sins,
giving us a new birth and
new life through the Holy Spirit.
He generously poured out the
Spirit upon us through Jesus Christ
our Savior. Because of His grace
He declared us righteous and
gave us confidence that we
will inherit eternal life.

Titus 3:5-7 NLT

GRACE

"I've redeemed you. I've called your name. You're Mine. When you're in over your head, I'll be there with you. That's how much you mean to Me! That's how much I love you! I'd sell off the whole world to get you back, trade the creation just for you."

Isaiah 43:1-2, 4 THE MESSAGE

"I will be your Father, and you will be My sons and daughters, says the Lord Almighty."

2 Corinthians 6:18 NCV

God is crazy about you.
He sends you flowers every spring
and a sunrise every morning.

~ Max Lucado

Little Miss Grace ...

Is Alive

Being made right with God by His grace,
we could have the hope of receiving
the life that never ends.

Titus 3:7 NCV

"Everyone who has faith in
the Son has eternal life."

John 3:36 CEV

Anyone who belongs to Christ has
become a new person. The old life
is gone; a new life has begun!

2 Corinthians 5:17 NLT

GRACE

"It is necessary for the Son of Man to be lifted up – and everyone who looks up to Him, trusting and expectant, will gain a real life, eternal life."

John 3:15 THE MESSAGE

I trust in Your unfailing love. I will rejoice because You have rescued me. I will sing to the LORD because He is good to me.

Psalm 13:5-6 NLT

GRACE

"God loved the people of this world so much that He gave His only Son, so that everyone who has faith in Him will have eternal life and never really die."

John 3:16 CEV

God has us where He wants us, with all the time in this world and the next to shower grace and kindness upon us in Christ Jesus. Saving is all His idea, and all His work. All we do is trust Him enough to let Him do it. It's God's gift from start to finish!

Ephesians 2:7-8 THE MESSAGE

"I know that eternal life comes from what the Father commands."

John 12:50 NCV

GRACE

To choose life is to love the Lord your God,
obey Him, and stay close to Him.
He is your life.

Deuteronomy 30:20 NCV

Even greater is God's wonderful grace and
His gift of righteousness, for all who receive
it will live in triumph over sin and death
through this one man, Jesus Christ.

Romans 5:17 NLT

God loves you so much that He never
wants to be separated from you.
That's why He created eternity —
so you could be with Him forever.

GRACE

Is Caring

The godly care for their animals.

Proverbs 12:10 NLT

The godly care about the
rights of the poor.

Proverbs 29:7 NLT

Love each other deeply
with all your heart.

1 Peter 1:22 NLT

Don't just pretend to love others.
Really love them.

Romans 12:9 NLT

GRACE

"Do to others whatever you would
like them to do to you."

Matthew 7:12 NLT

Jesus said, "Which one of these
three men do you think was a
neighbor to the man who was
attacked by the robbers?" The expert
on the law answered, "The one who
showed him mercy." Jesus said to him,
"Then go and do what he did."

Luke 10:36-37 NCV

GRACE

A sweet friendship
refreshes the soul.

Proverbs 27:9 THE MESSAGE

Anyone who loves another brother or
sister is living in the light and does not
cause others to stumble.

1 John 2:10 NLT

May the Lord make your love for
each other and for everyone else
grow by leaps and bounds.

1 Thessalonians 3:12 CEV

GRACE

If we love one another,
God dwells deeply within us,
and His love becomes
complete in us – perfect love!

1 John 4:12 THE MESSAGE

Caring for the poor is
lending to the LORD,
and you will be well repaid.

Proverbs 19:17 CEV

Live your life for others.

GRACE

Is Cheerful

A glad heart makes a happy face.

Proverbs 15:13 NLT

If you are cheerful, you feel good.

Proverbs 17:22 CEV

A cheerful look brings joy
to the heart.

Proverbs 15:30 NLT

A cheerful heart fills the day with song.

Proverbs 15:15 THE MESSAGE

Happy are the people whose God is the LORD.

Psalm 144:15 NCV

Young people, it's wonderful to be young!
Enjoy every minute of it. Do everything
you want to do; take it all in. But remember
that you must give an account to God
for everything you do.

Ecclesiastes 11:9 NLT

GRACE

The joy of the LORD will make you strong.

Nehemiah 8:10 NCV

You have shown me the path to life,
and You make me glad
by being near to me.
Sitting at Your right side,
I will always be joyful.

Psalm 16:11 CEV

The LORD has filled my heart with joy.

1 Samuel 2:1 NCV

Always be joyful.

1 Thessalonians 5:16 NCV

GRACE

Those who bring
sunshine to the lives
of others cannot keep
it from themselves.

~ James M. Barrie

GRACE

Is Confident

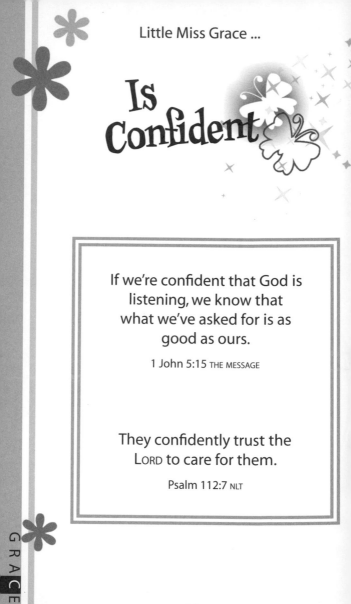

If we're confident that God is listening, we know that what we've asked for is as good as ours.

1 John 5:15 THE MESSAGE

They confidently trust the LORD to care for them.

Psalm 112:7 NLT

Blessed are those who
trust in the LORD and have made
the LORD their hope and confidence.

Jeremiah 17:7 NLT

Be strong and brave. Don't be afraid,
because the LORD your God will be
with you everywhere you go.

Joshua 1:9 NCV

GRACE

Be strong. Don't give up, because you will get a reward for your good work.

2 Chronicles 15:7 NCV

It's in Christ that we find out who we are and what we are living for.

Ephesians 1:11 THE MESSAGE

We thank God! He gives us the victory through our Lord Jesus Christ.

1 Corinthians 15:57 NCV

GRACE

You, LORD, are the light that keeps me safe.
I am not afraid of anyone.
You protect me, and I have no fears.

Psalm 27:1 CEV

The LORD will guard you as you come
and go, both now and forever.

Psalm 121:8 NCV

Having confidence in God means that you
will be able to do the unthinkable
and dream the unimaginable.

GRACE

Is Chosen by God

"Before I made you in your mother's womb, I chose you. Before you were born, I set you apart for a special work."

Jeremiah 1:5 NCV

The LORD says, "You are My witnesses and the servant I chose. I chose you so you would know and believe Me, so you would understand that I am the true God. There was no God before Me, and there will be no God after Me."

Isaiah 43:10 NCV

Before the world was created,
God had Christ choose us to live
with Him and to be His holy and
innocent and loving people.

Ephesians 1:4 CEV

Jesus said to His followers,
"Go everywhere in the world,
and tell the Good News to everyone."

Mark 16:15 NCV

You are God's chosen
and special people.

1 Peter 2:9 CEV

God raised us from death to life
with Christ Jesus, and He
has given us a place beside
Christ in heaven.

Ephesians 2:6 CEV

GRACE

God has given us the task
of telling everyone what He
is doing. We're Christ's
representatives.

2 Corinthians 5:19-20 THE MESSAGE

"You did not choose Me.
I chose you and sent you out
to produce fruit, the kind of fruit
that will last. Then My Father
will give you whatever you
ask for in My name."

John 15:16 CEV

For His own sake, the Lord won't leave His people. Instead, He was pleased to make you His own people.

1 Samuel 12:22 NCV

God saved us and called us to live a holy life. He did this, not because we deserved it, but because that was His plan from before the beginning of time – to show us His grace through Christ Jesus.

2 Timothy 1:9 NLT

God loves each one of us as if there were only one of us.

~ St. Augustine

Counts to Ten

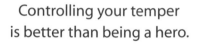

Controlling your temper
is better than being a hero.

Proverbs 16:32 CEV

It's wise to be patient and show
what you are like by forgiving others.

Proverbs 19:11 CEV

It's smart to be patient, but it's
stupid to lose your temper.

Proverbs 14:29 CEV

GRACE

A gentle answer will calm a person's anger,
but an unkind answer will cause more anger.

Proverbs 15:1 NCV

It is good to wait quietly.

Lamentations 3:26 NCV

Be patient and trust the LORD. Don't let it
bother you when all goes well for those
who do sinful things. Don't be angry
or furious. Anger can lead to sin.

Psalm 37:7-8 CEV

GRACE

With patience you can convince a ruler, and a gentle word can get through to the hard-headed.

Proverbs 25:15 NCV

Hot tempers start fights; a calm, cool spirit keeps the peace.

Proverbs 15:18 THE MESSAGE

Losing your temper is foolish; ignoring an insult is smart.

Proverbs 12:16 CEV

GRACE

Don't sin by letting anger control you.
Think about it overnight and remain silent.

Psalm 4:4 NLT

Don't get angry. Don't be upset;
it only leads to trouble.

Psalm 37:8 NCV

For every minute you
are angry you lose sixty
seconds of happiness.

~ Anonymous

Little Miss Grace ...

Is Content

Those who respect the LORD
will live and be satisfied.

Proverbs 19:23 NCV

Don't be obsessed with getting
more material things. Be relaxed
with what you have.

Hebrews 13:5 THE MESSAGE

Religion does make your life rich,
by making you content with
what you have.

1 Timothy 6:6 CEV

I am not complaining about having
too little. I have learned to be satisfied
with whatever I have.

Philippians 4:11 CEV

If they listen and obey God, they will be
blessed with prosperity throughout their
lives. All their years will be pleasant.

Job 36:11 NLT

You will keep in perfect peace all who trust in
You, all whose thoughts are fixed on You!

Isaiah 26:3 NLT

The Lord is my
shepherd; I have all
that I need. He lets me
rest in green meadows;
He leads me beside
peaceful streams.

Psalm 23:1-2 NLT

GRACE

"Be still, and know that I am God!"

Psalm 46:10 NLT

Be thankful in all circumstances, for this is God's will for you who belong to Christ Jesus.

1 Thessalonians 5:18 NLT

Keep your minds on whatever is true, pure, right, holy, friendly, and proper. Don't ever stop thinking about what is truly worthwhile and worthy of praise.

Philippians 4:8 CEV

Being content means
that you can find the joy
in everyday things — sharing
a giggle with your friend
or looking at a golden sunrise.

Encourages Others

Your love has given me much joy and comfort, for your kindness has often refreshed the hearts of God's people.

Philemon 1:7 NLT

Encourage each other and give each other strength, just as you are doing now.

1 Thessalonians 5:11 NCV

You must encourage one another each day.

Hebrews 3:13 CEV

GRACE

Everything that was written
in the past was written to teach us.
The Scriptures give us patience and
encouragement so that we can have hope.

Romans 15:4 NCV

Christ gives me the strength to
face anything.

Philippians 4:13 CEV

GRACE

When you talk, do not say harmful things,
but say what people need – words that
will help others become stronger.
Then what you say will do good
to those who listen to you.

Ephesians 4:29 NCV

Worry is a heavy load,
but a kind word cheers you up.

Proverbs 12:25 NCV

GRACE

Kind words please the LORD.

Proverbs 15:26 CEV

Kind words heal and help.

Proverbs 15:4 THE MESSAGE

Her words are sensible,
and her advice is thoughtful.

Proverbs 31:26 CEV

When you help others shine,
you can't help shining brightly too.

GRACE

Is Enthusiastic

Do your best.
Work from the heart for God.

Colossians 3:23 THE MESSAGE

Work hard, and you will be a leader.

Proverbs 12:24 CEV

Always give yourselves fully to
the work of the Lord, because you
know that your work in the
Lord is never wasted.

1 Corinthians 15:58 NCV

GRACE

The Lord your God will bless all the
work you do, and you will be
completely happy.

Deuteronomy 16:15 NCV

Be strong and courageous,
for your work will be rewarded.

2 Chronicles 15:7 NLT

She does her work with energy.

Proverbs 31:17 NCV

Depend on the Lord in whatever
you do, and your plans will succeed.

Proverbs 16:3 NCV

GRACE

117

Since we are surrounded by such a huge crowd of witnesses to the life of faith, let us strip off every weight that slows us down, especially the sin that so easily trips us up. And let us run with endurance the race God has set before us. We do this by keeping our eyes on Jesus, the Champion who initiates and perfects our faith.

Hebrews 12:1-2 NLT

GRACE

Those who trust the LORD
will find new strength.
They will be strong like eagles
soaring upward on wings;
they will walk and run
without getting tired.

Isaiah 40:31 CEV

Put your hope in the LORD.

Psalm 31:24 NCV

Life is what you make of it —
so make it good!

GRACE

Is Excited About the Future

"I say this because I know
what I am planning for you,"
says the LORD. "I have good plans
for you, not plans to hurt you.
I will give you hope and
a good future."

Jeremiah 29:11 NCV

If you do what the LORD wants,
He will make certain each step
you take is sure. The LORD will hold
your hand, and if you stumble,
you still won't fall.

Psalm 37:23-24 CEV

Trust God from the bottom
of your heart; don't try to figure out
everything on your own. Listen for
God's voice in everything you do,
everywhere you go; He's the one
who will keep you on track.

Proverbs 3:5-6 THE MESSAGE

The LORD will always guide you and
provide good things. He will make
you healthy. You will be like a garden
that has plenty of water or like a
stream that never runs dry.

Isaiah 58:11 CEV

You, LORD, are my God! I will praise
You for doing the wonderful things
You had planned and promised.

Isaiah 25:1 CEV

GRACE

I cry out to God who will fulfill
His purpose for me.

Psalm 57:2 NLT

The LORD will work out His plans for my life.

Psalm 138:8 NLT

With great wisdom You make plans,
and with Your great power You do all
the mighty things You planned.

Jeremiah 32:19 CEV

We know that God causes everything
to work together for the good of
those who love God and are called
according to His purpose for them.

Romans 8:28 NLT

Your life is a journey you must travel
with a deep consciousness of God.
You know you have a future in God.

1 Peter 1:18, 21 THE MESSAGE

GRACE

No eye has seen, no ear has heard,
and no mind has imagined what God
has prepared for those who love Him.

1 Corinthians 2:9 NLT

God planned for us to do good things and to
live as He has always wanted us to live. That's
why He sent Christ to make us what we are.

Ephesians 2:10 CEV

Your future is as bright as
the promises of God.

~ Adoniram Judson

Little Miss Grace ...

Is Eager to Obey

If you obey the laws and teachings that the LORD gave Moses, you will be successful. Be strong and brave and don't get discouraged or be afraid of anything.

1 Chronicles 22:13 CEV

"If you will obey Me and keep My covenant, you will be My own special treasure from among all the peoples on earth; for all the earth belongs to Me."

Exodus 19:5 NLT

Respect and obey the LORD! This is
the first step to wisdom and good sense.

Psalm 111:10 CEV

The LORD will withhold no good thing
from those who do what is right.

Psalm 84:11 NLT

Spend time with the wise and
you will become wise.

Proverbs 13:20 NCV

Each of you must show great respect
for your mother and father.

Leviticus 19:3 NLT

GRACE

Join the company of good men
and women, keep your feet on
the tried-and-true paths.

Proverbs 2:20 THE MESSAGE

Stand firm, and be strong in your faith.

1 Peter 5:9 NLT

Know that the LORD your God is God,
the faithful God. He will keep His
agreement of love for a thousand
lifetimes for people who love Him
and obey His commands.

Deuteronomy 7:9 NCV

"If you love Me, you will do as I
command. Then I will ask the Father
to send you the Holy Spirit who will
help you and always be with you.
The Spirit will show you what is true."

John 14:15-17 CEV

GRACE

Honor God and obey
His commands, because
this is all people must do.

Ecclesiastes 12:13 NCV

The LORD has told you, what is good;
He has told you what He wants from you:
to do what is right to other people,
love being kind to others,
and live humbly, obeying your God.

Micah 6:8 NCV

When we obey God, we open the
way for Him to bless us.

GRACE